THE SCIENCE OF
BUILDING A
RACING CAR

by

IAN GRAHAM

Consultant

BRYAN YAGER

ticktock
MEDIA

CONTENTS

Motor-racing makes use of the most advanced science, technology, materials and engineering to build the fastest cars. When the first race between cars was held in France in 1894, the winning car averaged a speed of 16.4 km/h. Since then, motor-racing teams have searched for every possible way of making their cars go faster.

THE SCIENCE OF SPEED

A team of people are involved in the science of creating fast car. Scientists called aerodynamicists design the shapes of racing cars. Chemists produce the **fuels** and oils used in their engines. Materials scientists are responsible for the advanced materials the cars are built from. Computer scientists develop the electronic systems that control the engines. They create the computer systems that are used to design the cars. Computers also enable the teams to test computerised versions of their cars. The forces that act on cars during a race are calculated by physicists and mathematicians. Engineers bring the work of all these scientists together to build the cars.

CHANGING THE RULES

Racing car designers are not able to use all the advances in materials, fuels, oils, computers, electronics and **aerodynamics** that they would like to, because they have to work within the rules of the sport. If the organisations that set the rules decide that cars are becoming too fast, they may change the rules to slow the cars down. If they see that some teams are spending huge sums of money on new technology that other teams can't afford, they may change the rules to make the competition fairer. Of all the different motor-sports, the rules of Formula 1 racing give its car designers the most freedom to use advanced science and technology.

NASCAR racing cars hug the track as they chase each other around a banked turn up to 300 km/h.

Brazilian driver Cristiano Da Matta sits in a Toyota at Silverstone during a Formula One Test session.

FROM TRACK TO ROAD

Some of the advanced science and technology used in racing cars are later built into ordinary cars to make them safer or more reliable. The types of brakes, tyres, some engine parts and some of the advanced materials found in ordinary family cars today were tested in racing cars first. The scientist's work in motor-racing is never finished, because people are constantly looking for new ways to make their cars go faster. The rules change every year, so the teams have to keep creating new cars. And new developments in science, technology, materials and engineering make new advances in car design possible.

Gary Scelzi sits in the cockpit of his dragster at the 39th Annual Pontiac Excitement Nationals at National Trail Raceway in Hebron, Ohio, USA.

Racing driver David Coulthard
squeezes into his super-slim car.

Racing cars go faster if they are the right shape, because some shapes slip through the air more easily than others. The scientific study of what happens to things when they move through air is called **aerodynamics**. Racing car designers use aerodynamics to find the right shape to make their cars.

BODY MATTERS

Racing cars have smooth, gently curving bodies to help them slip through the air. The body of a single-seat racing car is made very slim for the same reason. In fact, it's so slim that there is just enough room for the driver to wriggle down inside, but only if he takes the steering wheel off first! The car's body is slung low down between the wheels. It's so low that the driver has to lie on his back, driving feet-first.

SCIENCE CONCEPTS

DRAG

Drag is a force that slows a racing car down. When a car moves, it has to push the air out of its way. The air pushes back. Drag is the effect of the air pushing back against the car. It's also called **air resistance**. Some shapes produce more drag than others. A racing or sports car with a shape designed to produce very little drag, such as this Ferrari F50, is said to be streamlined.

A scale model of a Formula 1 car sits in a wind tunnel ready to be tested.

WINGS

Aerodynamicists add wings to racing cars so that they can take turns faster. If a racing car turns when it's going very fast, it risks sliding off the track. One way to stop it from skidding off is to push the wheels down harder, so the tyres grip the track better. Making the car heavier would do this, but it would also make the car slower. Valuable engine power would be wasted moving the extra weight. Wings do the same job without making the car much heavier. Aeroplanes use wings to lift them up into the air. Racing cars use upside-down wings to press them downwards. The effect of the wings is so powerful that a car could drive upside-down along the roof of a tunnel without falling off!

Wings enable cars to go round bends faster without skidding off the track.

AEROFOIL

The special shape of a wing is called an **aerofoil**. A racing car's wings are flatter on top and more curved underneath. As they cut through the air, air flowing underneath has to travel further across its curve than air flowing over the top. This causes suction under the wings and pulls the car downwards. This suction is also called **downforce**.

SCIENCE SNAPSHOT

The shapes of racing cars are tested in wind tunnels. A wind tunnel is a tube that air is blown through. Car designers started using them to test racing cars in the 1960s. Now, aerodynamics is so important that some motor-racing teams have their own wind tunnels. Some of them are so big that full-size racing cars can fit inside them, while others test smaller models of the cars.

An engine powers a car by burning **fuel** to release energy locked up inside. This energy is then used to turn the car's wheels. A racing car's engine is designed to change heat from burning fuel into movement as fast as possible – up to eight times faster than a family car's engine.

FIREPOWER

Engines work by burning fuel inside metal tubes called **cylinders**. **Formula 1** racing car engines have 10 cylinders. Most other racing cars have 8-cylinder engines. Air is sucked into each cylinder and fuel is added. Then a tight-fitting piston slides up the cylinder and squashes the mixture. An electric spark sets the fuel on fire, heating the air in the cylinder. The heat makes the air expand. The expanding air pushes the piston back down the cylinder with great force. The up-and-down movements, or **strokes**, of all the pistons provides the power to turn the car's wheels. The engine usually drives the two rear wheels in racing cars.

FUEL SCIENCE

Racing cars run on different types of fuel. While Formula 1 racing cars burn **petrol**, **Champ** cars and **Indy Racing**

This Formula 1 engine racing engine was used in the 1999 season . It has ten cylinders, five on each side, to provide the enormous amount of power needed.

SCIENCE CONCEPTS

COMBUSTION

Combustion, another name for burning, is a chemical reaction between a gas and air that gives out heat and light. To get the best performance from a racing car's engine, the fuel and air must mix together so that the fuel burns quickly. Scientists design the shape inside the tops of the cylinders very carefully so that it stirs up the air and fuel as they come into the engine.

This Porsche sports car is powered by a turbocharged engine.

League cars burn a fuel called **methanol**. Methanol is one single chemical, but **petrol** is a complicated mixture of different chemicals. Chemists can produce different mixtures, or blends, of petrol to suit different engines and even different race-tracks. The leading Formula 1 racing teams have their own fuel scientists who work to produce the right fuel for their cars.

SLIPPERY CHEMISTRY

All the time an engine is running, oil flows through it to make its moving parts slippery. The slippery parts slide across each other easily without sticking. Oil is especially important to racing car engines, because they work up to three times faster than a family car engine. Every time a racing car is driven, scientists test a little of its engine oil. Tiny metal specks found in the oil tell them how fast the engine's moving parts are wearing away and if anything is going wrong inside.

SCIENCE SNAPSHOT

Fuel will burn only when it is mixed with air. An engine can be made to burn more fuel by forcing extra air into it. Burning more fuel makes the engine more powerful and the car faster. A machine called a turbocharger blows more air into an engine. Champ cars and many road cars like this Porsche are powered by turbocharged engines.

A racing car's tyres are the car's only link with the ground. Their job is to change the engine's immense power into speed. To do that, they have to grip the ground without skidding or sliding. They also have to withstand the ferocious forces that try to tear them apart during a race. Scientists have developed new types of rubber specially for racing cars.

Scientists make the rubber for racing car tyres from more than 100 ingredients.

BIG AT THE BACK

Most racing cars have bigger, wider wheels at the back and smaller wheels at the front. The reason is that the rear wheels are driven by the engine and so it is important that they grip the ground when the engine turns them. Bigger, wider tyres put more rubber on the ground and so give more grip, especially in turns. The front wheels are made smaller to help the car's **aerodynamics**. Smaller wheels at the front cause less **drag**.

SCIENCE CONCEPTS

FRICTION

Friction is a force that enables a racing car's tyres to grip the ground. It tries to stop things sliding against each other. There is more friction between surfaces when they are rougher or pressed together harder. There is less friction if the surfaces are smoother or wet. Racing cars are more likely to skid on a wet track, because water reduces the friction between the tyres and the track.

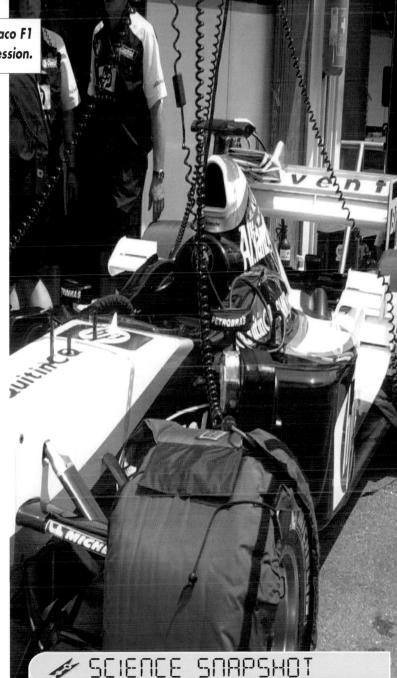

BMW Williams tyre warmers on a car during 2003 Monaco F1 Grand Prix practice session.

RACING RUBBER

Racing tyres are made of a special type of a rubber. It is softer and stickier than normal tyres. The soft, sticky rubber grips the ground better, but it has a disadvantage. Racing car tyres wear away faster than normal tyres. While a family car's tyres last for tens of thousands of kilometres, a **Formula 1** racing car's tyres last only about 200 km!

Racing cars are fitted with tyres to suit the weather conditions during a race. It is vital to get the choice of tyres right.

The drivers must stop during the race at their team's garage in the 'pits' by the side of the track and have the car's wheels changed before the rubber breaks up completely.

CHANGING WEATHER, CHANGING TYRES

Slicks (smooth tyres) put the most rubber in contact with the ground and so create the most grip, but only on a dry track. If a track is wet, water gets between the tyres and the track and the tyres lose grip, so **'wets'** (wet-weather tyres) are used. They squish water out from under the tyres through channels and keep the tyres in contact with the ground.

SCIENCE SNAPSHOT

As a car is driven along, its tyres heat up. The rubber that racing tyres are made from is designed to give the most grip when it's hot. It works best at a temperature of about 100°C – hot enough to boil water! Just before a race, Formula 1 teams wrap their wheels in electric blankets to heat the tyres up to the right temperature, so they give lots of grip from the start. And when a car needs new tyres during a race, the new wheels are heated up before they are fitted.

Racing cars are made from a variety of different materials. Some of them are traditional materials such as steel, but materials scientists and chemists have provided car designers with new materials that are lighter and stronger. It is important to save weight, because a lighter car **accelerates** faster than a heavier car.

CARBON FIBRE

Racing cars used to be made from steel, but today most racing cars have replaced nearly all of the steel with a material called **carbon fibre**. More than four-fifths of a **Formula 1** racing car is made from carbon fibre. It is used because it's a quarter the weight of steel and also twice as strong.

It is made from long thread-like fibres of carbon woven together to form mats. The mats are soaked in

Carbon fibre cars are all black, but are painted with the team's colour scheme.

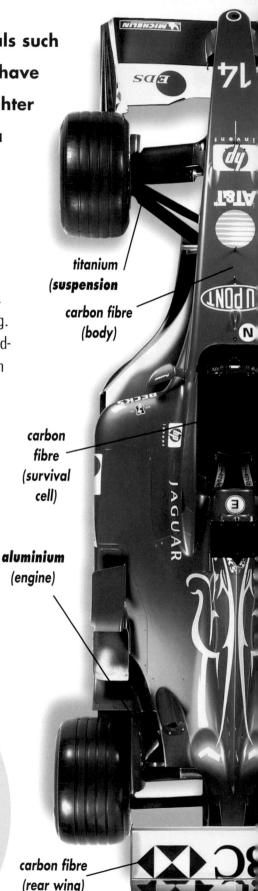

titanium (suspension

carbon fibre (body)

carbon fibre (survival cell)

aluminium (engine)

carbon fibre (rear wing)

⊜ SCIENCE CONCEPTS

POLYMERS

Carbon fibre is a type of material called a **polymer** (see left). There are lots of polymers in nature. Diamond, natural rubber and some parts of plants are polymers. Substances called proteins in our body are polymers. Scientists can make polymers by adding lots of simple chemical units called monomers together to form long chains. Polymers made in laboratories include nylon, polythene, polystyrene, PVC and carbon fibre.

rbon fibre (nose cone)

agnesium
(wheels)

rubber
(tyres)

> *Some of the metal parts of a racing car are connected together by welding - melting their edges together.*

a liquid plastic, called resin. While the resin is liquid, the mats can be moulded into any shape. Then the resin sets hard, forming a solid, lightweight material. To ensure that it sets in exactly the right way, the parts are baked at a carefully controlled temperature in a special oven called an autoclave. Carbon fibre is strong enough to be used to make a racing car's **chassis**, the main frame that provides the car's strength. The rest of the car is built on the chassis. Its nose and wings are made from carbon fibre too.

SITTING IN A BATHTUB

The driver of a single-seat racing car is surrounded by carbon fibre. He sits inside a super-strong compartment called the **survival cell**. Because of its shape, it is also known as the '**bath-tub**'. The **survival cell** is designed to withstand the most serious crash a racing car may suffer. It is made from a 'sandwich' of materials — carbon fibre on the outside, with a very lightweight filling made from **aluminium** honeycomb. The filling makes it light and the carbon fibre makes it strong. The survival cell has to pass a series of cash tests to prove it is strong enough before it is allowed to be used on a race-track.

⚡ SCIENCE SNAPSHOT

Slicks (smooth tyres) put the most rubber in contact with the ground and so create the most grip, but only on a dry track If a track is wet, water gets between the tyres and the track and the tyres lose grip, so 'wets' (wet-weather tyres) are used. They squish water out from under the tyres through channels and keep the tyres in contact with the ground.

In the past, the only way a motor-racing team could find out how well a car was running during a race was to ask the driver afterwards. Nowadays, teams receive information from cars during a race by radio. If all the information sent from each **Formula 1** racing car during a race was printed out on paper, the pile of pages would be as tall as the Empire State Building!

A driver's helmet contains a radio microphone and earpieces.

On-board cameras show television viewers exactly what a racing driver can see during a race.

⊜ SCIENCE CONCEPTS

RADIO SIGNALS

The radio signals that carry information about racing cars are made of electric and magnetic vibrations travelling at the speed of light – 300,000 kilometres per second! Their great speed means that information travels from a car to its team at the track-side in an instant. If a sensor in a car detects a problem, the information appears on the team's computer screens within a tenth of a second!

COLLECTING DATA

Dozens of measurements are taken from all over a racing car, including the engine speed, temperature, wheel speed and even the air pressure inside the tyres. This information is sent by radio to the teams at the track-side, where it appears on their computer screens. Taking measurements at a distance like this is called **telemetry**. It enables technicians to spot a problem before the driver feels anything wrong with the car. The team can then tell the driver to slow down or stop before the car breaks down or suffers an accident.

Information from racing cars can be downloaded into computers and viewed on their screens.

COCKPIT PICTURES

Video cameras are so small now that they can be fitted to racing cars to give television viewers a driver's-eye view of a race. Pictures from the cameras are transmitted by radio to a track-side receiver. If one of the cameras picks up something interesting, its pictures are shown on television. Pictures from on-board cameras are also very useful for finding out how an accident may have occurred. Accidents are often filmed by a following car. The close-up pictures may reveal something that people and cameras further away didn't see.

SPLIT-SECOND TIMING

Racing cars often cross the finish line so close together that they have to be timed to within one thousandth of a second. A few races are so closely fought that they have to be timed to within one ten-thousandth of a second. Only electronic timing is capable of this level of accuracy. Each car transmits its own code number. **Sensor**s buried under the track pick up the codes as the cars pass over them. Other systems, including high-speed cameras at the finish line double-check the results.

⚐ SCIENCE SNAPSHOT

*The devices fitted to racing cars to identify them are called **transponders**. Transponder is short for transmitter-responder. A transponder is a small box of electronics about the size of a pocket calculator. It sends out a coded radio signal that tells the timing system at the race-track which car is which.*

A racing car can **accelerate**, brake and steer in a controlled way only when its tyres touch the ground. That means the wheels have to follow all the bumps and dips in the ground. If the whole car did that, it would shake so much it would be very hard to drive. Cars are designed so that the wheels can spring up and down, but the body glides along more smoothly.

SUSPENSION

A car's body is supported, or suspended, by a set of springs and other devices called the **suspension** system. If the wheels and body were linked together by springs alone, the car would bounce up and down too much as it sped along a bumpy track. To stop this happening, the suspension springs are fitted with devices called dampers or shock absorbers. They let the springs squash down fast, to soak up bumps on the track, but make them spring back more slowly.

RIDE HEIGHT

Racing cars are designed to be very close to the ground. The distance between the ground and the bottom of the car's body is called its **ground clearance** or **ride height**. A single-seat racing car's body is only

Racing cars are designed to stick to the track in turns at speed that would have an ordinary car spinning off.

2-3 centimetres above the ground. It's made this low so that most of the air it pushes out of the way as it speeds along the track has to go over the top of the car, where the body and wings use it to produce **downforce**.

SETTING UP

Racing cars are adjusted, or 'set up', specially for each race. One of the most important settings to get right is the angle, or tilt, of the wings. Another is the suspension. A family car's suspension lets the car move up and down quite a lot, because it's more comfortable. Racing cars aren't made for comfort. They have a much harder suspension. It can be adjusted to make it even harder or a little softer to suit each race-track. Even the weather forecast for the day of a race can change the way the team adjusts the suspension.

SCIENCE CONCEPTS

SPRINGS

When you bend or squash a spring, you use energy. The spring stores this energy. When you let go, the spring releases the energy again. A racing car's suspension springs do the same thing. Every time a wheel is bumped upwards by rough ground, its suspension spring is squashed. It soaks up the energy of the bump and then releases it again when the wheel drops back down.

Racing cars have to cope with all sorts of track and road surfaces.

SCIENCE SNAPSHOT

When a car takes a turn, it rolls to one side and when the driver brakes hard its nose dips. But a racing car's aerodynamics work perfectly only when the car is level. A system called active suspension constantly adjusts itself to keep the car level all the time. Active suspension was used in Formula 1, but it is not allowed now.

Computers and electronics monitor every part of a racing car to make sure the car always performs at its best. Computers can sense changes in the way the car is working and react to them far faster than a human driver can. Computers can also test parts of cars and whole racing cars by using computer programs called simulations.

COMPUTER SIMULATIONS

Some motor-racing computer games look very realistic. Real racing cars are tested in the same way.
A computer is programmed with a model of a car or just part of the car. The computer can then show how air flows around it or how forces acting on it change at different speeds or in turns. Whole race tracks can be copied, or modelled, in a computer. Computer-

Without traction control, a car's wheels spin too fast, creating smoke in this case.

generated cars are raced around the track to try out different ways of adjusting, or setting up, a car for a race. These computer programs and the tests they run are called **computer simulations**, because they copy, or simulate, the real thing.

⊕ SCIENCE CONCEPTS

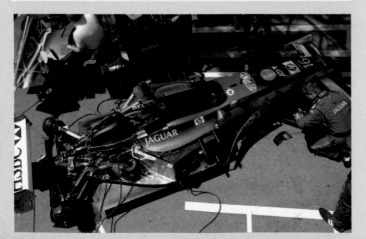

SENSORS

Sensors all over a racing car collect information about the car and how well it is working. A Formula 1 car has more than 100 sensors. They detect changes in the temperature, pressure and speed of various parts of the car and change them into electric currents. In this form, the information is easier to move from place to place along wires or by radio, and to process by computer.

Drivers line their cars up on the starting grid for a race. They all want to get away from the start-line as fast as possible.

COMPUTER CONTROL

A racing car's engine is controlled by a box of electronics called the engine management system (EMS) or engine control unit (ECU). When the driver presses the car's **accelerator** pedal, the engine controller senses how the pedal is moving and controls the engine so that it does what the driver wants. The engine controller is programmed differently to suit different race tracks.

TRACTION CONTROL

Traction is another word for the grip between a car's tyres and the ground. If a driver accelerates too quickly, the engine is so powerful that it can spin the wheels too fast. Wheel-spin breaks the grip between the tyres and the track and wastes engine power. An electronic **traction control** system senses when wheels are about to spin too fast. It takes over control of the engine and stops wheel-spin before it starts. Traction control is especially important in wet weather, when wheel-spin is more likely to happen. Traction control is not allowed in most types of motor-racing.

Programming a racing car's engine control unit is an important part of preparing the car for the next race.

✦ SCIENCE SNAPSHOT

Drivers sometimes make mistakes at the beginning of a race. The car's wheels may spin and lose grip or the engine may stop. An electronic system called **launch control** can produce a perfect start every time. It feeds engine power to the wheels in exactly the right way. Launch control is not allowed in most motor-sports. It was used in Formula 1 racing until 2004.

Racing cars are now designed so that their wheels can't fly off and hurt anyone after an accident.

Motor-racing drivers often walk away unhurt from accidents that people in ordinary cars would not survive. Physicists study the forces and energy involved in crashes. This information is used to design cars that soak up the impact of a crash and save the driver. One of the greatest dangers in motor-racing is fire, but safety features built into racing cars today make them less likely to catch fire.

CRUSH ZONES

If a racing car was made super-strong all over, it would stop in an instant if it hit something. Stopping a car so suddenly would produce incredibly powerful forces that a driver might not survive. Some parts of a racing car are designed to be crushed in a crash. These parts, mainly in the nose and tail, are called crush zones. As they collapse, they soak up some of the car's energy and it takes a fraction of a second longer to come to a stop. The forces acting on the driver's body are reduced and the driver is more likely to survive a serious accident.

A driver makes a quick exit from his racing car after its engine catches fire.

SCIENCE CONCEPTS

G-FORCES

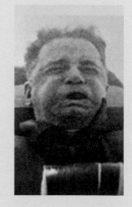

The forces experienced by racing cars and drivers are called g-forces. A force of 2g is twice as strong as the force of gravity, 3g is three times the force of gravity and so on. You feel g-forces when a car **accelerates**, brakes or turns a corner. A racing driver feels a force of about 5g in a turn. In the most serious head-on crashes, a driver may experience 50-100g! In the picture on the right, the subject is experiencing the uncomfortable effects of extreme g-forces.

Today's Formula 1 racing cars have built-in fire extinguishers that are automatically set off if the car crashes and catches fire.

FLYING WHEELS

Parts of cars that break off during a crash can be very dangerous. In the past, drivers and people watching races have been hurt and even killed by wheels that came off cars and flew through the air. Most racing cars now have to be built so that their wheels can't fly off. Super-strong ropes, called tethers, tie the wheels to the car's body.

FUEL CELL

Some parts of a racing car get very hot during a race. Parts of the brakes get so hot that they glow bright red! If **fuel** was spilt on them, it would burst into flames. It is very important to stop fuel from leaking, especially after an accident. A racing car's fuel is kept in a flexible bag, called a **fuel cell**, made from the same material as bullet-proof vests. If a car crashes, the bag can squash down and change shape without springing a leak. The car's fuel pipes are also fitted with valves that automatically snap shut to stop fuel from leaking out.

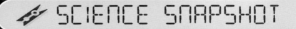

SCIENCE SNAPSHOT

Racing cars are fitted with fire extinguishers that spray foam into the engine compartment and cockpit. The chemical foam is designed to cover a fire and cut off the oxygen it needs. Without oxygen from the surrounding air, the fire quickly dies.

Formula 1 is the world's biggest and most popular international motor-sport. Hundreds of millions of people watch each race on television. Its rules give teams a lot of freedom to use advanced science and technology in their cars. But the cost of designing, building and racing these cars is enormous. A successful team may have more than 300 people working for it and spend more than £200 million pounds a year!

AERODYNAMICS

The shape of every part of a Formula 1 car is designed to reduce **air resistance** as much as possible and produce the most **downforce**. Even the shape of the driver's helmet is designed to smooth out the air flowing over the car's cockpit. In a fast turn, a driver can feel a sideways force of up to five times the force of gravity. That means the driver's body feels as if it weighs a third of a tonne! Drivers have to be very fit and strong to cope with such powerful forces throughout a race.

The shape of a driver's helmet affects the air-flow over an open cockpit, so helmets are tested in wind tunnels to get their shape right.

This well-worn Formula 1 tyre shows the four grooves that all Formula 1 dry-weather tyres must have.

A Formula 1 racing engine is eight times as powerful as a family car engine, but is less than half its weight.

THE POWER OF V

Formula 1 racing cars are powered by 3-litre V10 engines. Three litres is the size of the space inside the **cylinders**, where the **fuel** is burned. It's called a V10 engine, because it has 10 cylinders arranged in two rows of five joined at the bottom, forming the shape of a letter V. At full speed, each of the ten pistons inside the engine goes up and down 300 times a second!

GROOVY TYRES

Formula 1 cars used to run on completely smooth tyres called **slicks** on dry tracks. To stop the cars from going round turns too fast, the rules were changed and slick tyres were banned. Now, Formula 1 dry-weather tyres must have four grooves cut in them. The **grooved slicks** mean there is less rubber touching the track. With a little less grip, the drivers can't take turns so fast. When a Formula 1 car is hurtling along a track at full speed, its wheels turn more than 40 times per second!

CASE STUDY FACTFILE

The Formula 1 world championship began in 1950 Today the F1 championship is run over about 16 races. The races are help mainly in Europe. Each Formula 1 racing car is made from about 9,000 parts.

FORMULA 1 CAR

Top speed:	*360 km/h*
Engine:	*3-litre V10*
Fuel:	*petrol*
Power:	*900 horsepower*
Weight:	*at least 600kg including the driver*
Length:	*up to 4.2m*
Width:	*up to 1.8m*
Height:	*up to 95cm*

The famous Indianapolis Raceway has hosted F1 races in the USA.

NASCAR racing cars are called stock cars, because they used to be stock (ordinary) cars that anyone could buy. Ordinary cars didn't last long on racetracks before something broke, so teams fitted them with stronger parts from trucks. Steel cages were built inside them to stop the roof collapsing if they turned over. More changes were made over the years. Today, they still look like ordinary cars, but they're built specially for racing.

NASCAR drivers are kitted out with full safety gear.

CONSTRUCTION

A NASCAR racing car starts as a pile of steel sheets and steel tubes. The tubes are welded together to form a frame. The front and back are made from weaker, thinner tubes than the middle of the car, where the driver sits. In a crash, the weaker nose and tail are designed to crush first, soaking up some of the energy of the crash and protecting the driver. The car's metal skeleton is covered with sheets of steel, cut and shaped to form the body.

POWER

The engine is fitted at the front, driving the rear wheels. For maximum safety, the engine is designed be pushed downwards through the bottom of the car in a head-on crash instead of backwards into the driver's seat. A thick metal plate called a **firewall** between the engine and the driver stops a fire in the engine spreading into the driver's compartment.

The Plymouth Superbird, a favourite NASCR competitor in the early 1970s, sports a high rear wing.

STAYING ON THE GROUND

If a NASCAR car spins around, the same shape that makes it hug the ground when going forwards acts like a wing if it goes tail first. If it's going fast enough, it may actually take off and fly through the air! The cars are now fitted with flaps on their roof to stop this happening. If a car spins around backwards, the flaps automatically pop up. They change the car's shape, so that it doesn't act like a wing and doesn't take off.

NASCAR races are always keenly fought, exciting races between closely matched cars.

A NASCAR racing car's doors don't open. The driver gets in and out through the side window! The window is covered with a net to stop anything flying in, or the driver's arms flying out, during a crash.

NASCAR car

Top speed:	*320 km/h*
Engine:	*5.8-litre V8*
Fuel:	*petrol*
Power:	*750 horsepower*
Weight:	*at least 1,540kg without the driver*
Length:	*5.1m*
Width:	*up to 2.0m*
Height:	*up to 1.3m*

A car's tail slides out on a fast turn and smoke billows from the tyres.

The two main types of single-seat racing in the USA are **CART** Champ car racing and the **Indy Racing League** (IRL). Champ cars are the world's fastest racing cars. They're sometimes called America's Formula 1, and they look like Formula 1 cars, but they're quite different. They have different engines that burn different fuel.

ENGINES

Champ cars have smaller engines than Formula 1 cars. They use a **turbocharger** to boost their power. The **turbocharger** is like a super-powerful fan that blows extra air inside the engine. If it tries to blow in more air than the rules allow, a valve opens like a tap and lets the extra air out. It's called a pop-off valve, because when it opens it makes a loud popping sound. The pop-off valves makes sure that the engines used by all the different cars are evenly matched.

FUEL

Champ car engines burn **methanol** instead of **petrol**. **Methanol** was chosen for safety reasons. A methanol fire is easy to put out by throwing water on it, because water mixes with methanol. Water doesn't mix with petrol. Petrol will float on top of water. And when water hits burning petrol, it can change to steam and expand so fast that it sprays burning petrol in all directions. One disadvantage of methanol is that it burns with an invisible flame, so **fuel** spilled on a car could catch fire without anyone noticing. Only someone close enough to feel the heat can tell there's a fire.

*A Champ car can **accelerate** from the start-line to 100 km/g in less than two and a half seconds!*

An experienced pit team can change a car's wheels and re-fuel it within a few seconds.

CHAMP V FORMULA 1

If a Champ Car and a Formula 1 car were to race against each other on a straight level track, the Champ car would win, because it's the fastest in a straight line. But on a circuit with left and right turns, nothing can beat the best Formula 1 cars.

Oval circuits give spectators a great view of the race

CASE STUDY FACTFILE

Champ Cars
Champ cars burn fuel so fast that they go only about 850 metres on every litre of methanol.

CART Champ car

Top speed:	*380 km/h*
Engine:	*2.65-litre V-8 turbocharged*
Fuel:	*methanol*
Power:	*750 horsepower*
Weight:	*at least 709kg without the driver (699kg at superspeedway races)*
Length:	*4.83-4.98m*
Width:	*up to 2.0m*
Height:	*up to 81cm*

IRL cars

IRL cars have bigger methanol-burning engines than Champ cars, but without turbochargers to boost their power, they are less powerful.

Top speed:	*370 km/h*
Engine:	*3.5-litre V8*
Fuel:	*methanol*
Power:	*650 horsepower*
Weight:	*at least 690kg without fuel and driver*
Length:	*4.83-4.95m*
Width:	*up to 2.0m*
Height:	*up to 96.5cm*

designed for racing and they are very different from their road-going cousins.

BODY AND SHAPE

A sports car designed for racing usually has its engine in the middle of the car, behind the driver. The engine is the heaviest part of the car. Putting it in the middle makes the car steadier and easier to handle. It also puts the heavy engine closer to the wheels it drives, so that its weight presses the wheels against the ground and helps to give the tyres more grip.

Its streamlined body is designed to slip through the air easily and produce lots of **downforce** so that it can take turns faster. Some of these cars have a wing at the back to produce even more downforce.

The driver sits to one side of the car. Sports cars have two seats, for a driver and passenger. Even though racing sports cars never carry a passenger, they still have to have a space for a passenger seat.

This Porsche sports car has had a rear wing added for racing.

At top speed, the Audi R8 is three times faster than a family car!

24 HOURS AT THE WHEEL

The toughest test for racing sports cars is an endurance race. Endurance races last up to 24 hours. The most famous of these is the race at Le Mans in France. In 24 hours, the fastest cars make nearly 400 laps of the circuit and cover a distance of more than 5,000km. A team of drivers shares the driving. Unlike most other racing cars, these cars have headlights, because they carry on racing at top speed all through the night.

Audi R8 drivers celebrate winning the 24 hours Le Mans race in 2001.

AUDI R8

One of the most successful sports racing cars in recent years is the Audi R8. It won the Le Mans 24-hour race in 2000, 2001, 2002 and 2004. It's a type of car called a Le Mans Prototype, or LMP900. These cars have an open cockpit and they must weigh at least 900kg. They are allowed to have an engine of up to 6.0 litres in size, or 4.0 litres turbocharged. The Audi R8's 3.6-litre turbocharged engine can boost it from a standstill to 100 km/h in less than 3.5 seconds. A family car takes up to 10 seconds or more to do the same thing.

CASE STUDY FACTFILE

AUDI R8 SPORTS RACING CAR

Top speed: 330 km/h
Engine: 3.6-litre V8 turbocharged
Fuel: petrol
Power: 600 horsepower
Weight: at least 900kg
Length: 4.65m
Width: 2.0m
Height: 1.08m

The Charparral sports car (white) pioneered the use of wings in the late 1960s.

Acceleration Scientists use the word acceleration to mean any change in speed or direction, but outside the laboratory most people use acceleration to mean going faster.

Aerodynamics The scientific study of what happens when an object moves through air, or when air moves around an object.

Aerofoil The special shape of a wing, which produces a force at right angles to its direction of travel. Aircraft use wings to produce an upwards force called lift. Racing cars use upside-down wings to produce a downwards force called downforce.

Air resistance A force that tries to slow down a moving car, caused by air pushing against a car as it tries to move. Another name for air resistance is drag.

Aluminium A metal used in the construction of racing cars because of its light weight. Aluminium is the third commonest element in the Earth's crust.

Bath-tub Another name for a single-seat racing car's survival cell, the super-strong compartment where the driver sits.

Carbon fibre A very strong and lightweight material made from a hard resin strengthened by long strands, or fibres, of carbon. The fibres are usually woven into mats. Materials like carbon fibre, made from two or more different materials, are called composites.

CART Championship Auto Racing Teams, the organisation that controls and regulates Champ car racing in the USA.

Chassis A car's main frame. The rest of the car is built on the chassis (pronounced 'shassee').

Combustion Another word for burning, a chemical reaction between a gas and air, producing light and heat.

Computer simulation A copy, or model, of a racing car, or part of a racing car, or a whole race that is created in a computer and appears on the computer's screen.

Cylinder The tube-shaped part of an engine where the fuel is burned. Most racing cars have engines with eight or ten cylinders.

Downforce A downwards force acting on a racing car, produced by its wings and the shape of its body.

Drag Another name for air resistance, a force that acts on a racing car when it moves through air, caused by the air pushing back against the car.

Firewall A sheet of metal or other material designed to stop fire spreading from one part of a racing car to another part.

Formula A set of rules for motor-racing. The best-known type of formula racing is Formula 1.

Formula 1 The leading international motor-racing championship.

Fuel A material burned to produce heat or power. Anything that burns can be used as a fuel. Petrol and methanol are used as fuels in motor-racing.

Fuel cell A tough, flexible bag that holds a racing car's fuel.

Grooved slick A type of tyre used in Formula 1 motor-racing, which is smooth apart from grooves cut in the rubber.

Ground clearance The distance between the ground and the bottom of a racing car's body. Also called ride height.

Ground effect The suction that pulls a racing car downwards, produced by the shape of the car's body and wings.

Horsepower A unit of power, used to measure how powerful car engines are.

Indy Racing League One of the single-seat motor-racing sports in the USA.

Launch control An electronic system designed to give a racing car a perfect start.

Magnesium A type of metal used in the construction of racing cars, because of its light weight.

Methanol A type of alcohol used as fuel by some racing cars. Also called methyl alcohol or wood alcohol.

NASCAR The National Association for Stock Car Auto Racing. The organisation that controls stock car racing in the USA.

Petrol A fuel made from crude oil, or petroleum. Also called gasoline.

Polymer A material made from long chains of small chemical units called monomers. Plastics including polythene and PVC are made from polymers.

Ride height The distance between the ground and the bottom of a racing car's body. Also called ground clearance.

Sensor A device that detects matter, force or energy.

Slick A smooth tyre used by some racing cars on dry race-tracks.

Stroke A movement of a piston inside a cylinder in a car engine.

Survival cell The super-strong compartment in a single-seat racing car where the driver sits. Also called the bath-tub.

Suspension The springs and other devices between a car's body and wheels that let the wheels follow bumps and dips in the road while the car's body moves along more smoothly.

Telemetry Taking measurements at a distance. Sensors in a racing car take measurements from all over the car and its engine and then send the measurements by radio to the team at the track-side.

Traction Another word for grip between a racing car's tyres and the ground.

Traction control An electronic system designed to stop a racing car's wheels spinning too fast and losing grip.

Transponder A device that transmits a coded radio signal identifying the racing car carrying the device.

Turbocharger A device added to an engine to force more air inside it, so that it can burn more fuel and produce more power. Some racing cars have turbocharged engines.

Wets Wet-weather tyres used in motor racing.

Copyright © ticktock Entertainment Ltd 2004
First published in Great Britain in 2004 by ticktock Media Ltd.,
Unit 2, Orchard Business Centre, North Farm Road, Tunbridge Wells, Kent, TN2 3XF
We would like to thank: Jenni Rainford for their help with this book.
ISBN 1 86007 589 4 HB   ISBN 1 86007 583 5 PB
Printed in China
A CIP catalogue record for this book is available from the British Library.

Picture Credits
Action Plus: 2-3c, 4-5 all, 7r, 8c, 12l, 14tr, 14bl, 15t, 15c, 18c, 18b, 19r, 22l, 28-29c, 29t. Alamy: 12bl, 28l, 29br. Car Photo Library:
6bl. Motoring Picture Library: 6-7c, 10-11c. Redzone: 10b, 20tl, 23bc, 23br, 26-27c, 27b. Science Photo Library: 13r, 20bl & br.
Sporting Images: 6tl, 8b, 10tl, 11r, 12c, 16c, 17c, 20-21c, 21r, 23t, 24-25c, 25br, 26b.